Date: 4/22/14

J 594.3 BAX
Baxter, Bethany.
Conches /

AWESOME ARMORED ANIMALS

CONCHES

Bethany Baxter

PowerKiDS press™

New York

Published in 2014 by The Rosen Publishing Group, Inc.
29 East 21st Street, New York, NY 10010

First Edition

Editor: Julia Quinlan
Book Design: Greg Tucker

Photo Credits: Cover Stephen Frink/Digital Vision/Getty Images; p. 4 Alex James Bramwell/Shutterstock.com; p. 5 Michael Lawrence/Lonely Planet Images/Getty Images; p. 6 Ecostock/Shutterstock.com; p. 7 Holger Wulschlaeger/Shutterstock.com; p. 8 mrclark321/iStockPhoto.com; p. 9 Michael Gerber/Flickr/Getty Images; p. 10 Reinhard Dirscherl/Visuals Unlimited/Getty Images; p. 11 Charles V. Angelo/Photo Researchers/Getty Images; pp. 12–13 Andrew J. Martinez/Photo Researchers/Getty Images; p. 14 Vanilla Fire/Shutterstock.com; pp. 15 (top), 22 Peter Leahy/Shutterstock.com; p. 15 (bottom) iofoto/Shutterstock.com; p. 16 MP cz/Shutterstock.com; p. 17 Stephan Kerkhofs/Shutterstock.com; p. 18 Brian J. Skerry/National Geographic/Getty Images; p. 19 Rich Carey/Shutterstock.com; p. 20 mikeledray/Shutterstock.com; p. 21 Michele Westmorland/Photodisc/Getty Images.

Library of Congress Cataloging-in-Publication Data

Baxter, Bethany.
 Conches / by Bethany Baxter. — First edition.
    pages cm. — (Awesome armored animals)
 Includes index.
 ISBN 978-1-4777-0796-8 (library binding) — ISBN 978-1-4777-0964-1 (pbk.) — ISBN 978-1-4777-0965-8 (6-pack)
 1. Strombidae—Juvenile literature. I. Title.
 QL430.5.S8B39 2014
 594'.3—dc23
                              2013000196

Manufactured in the United States of America

CPSIA Compliance Information: Batch #S13PK6: For Further Information contact Rosen Publishing, New York, New York at 1-800-237-9932

Contents

Shell Armor

Conches are **marine** snails. They live in warm ocean waters all over the world. Conches have large **spiral** shells. These hard shells act like armor to keep their soft bodies safe from **predators**.

Conches are part of a large group of marine animals called mollusks. Other mollusks include clams, oysters, octopi, and squid.

Conch shells come in many different colors. This is a queen conch.

Conches have two eyes
inside of their shells.

Snails and slugs form a smaller group of mollusks
called **gastropods**. True conches are snails in their
own **family** of gastropods.

One of the best-known conches is the queen conch.
Other conches include the milk conch, the rooster tail
conch, the spider conch, and the fighting conch.

Warm, Shallow Waters

Conches live in tropical water **habitats**. Most conches can be found in the warm waters of the Indian Ocean and the western and central Pacific Ocean. This area is called the Indo-Pacific. Other conches live in parts of the Atlantic Ocean, Caribbean Sea, and Mediterranean Sea.

Conches live on the seafloor. This queen conch is sitting on the sandy bottom of the Caribbean Sea, near the Cayman Islands.

The waters of the Caribbean Sea are nice and warm, which is perfect for conches.

Conches are bottom-dwellers. They make their homes in sand, gravel, beds of sea grass, and coral reefs on the ocean floor.

Queen conches live in **shallow** waters throughout the Caribbean Sea and the Gulf of Mexico. They can be found in waters between 1 foot and 70 feet deep (.3 m–21.3 m).

Hard Outside, Soft Inside

Conches are invertebrates. This means they do not have backbones inside their bodies. Instead, they have hard outer shells. The shells are spiral-shaped. Conches are born with their shells.

A conch grows its shell using an **organ** called a mantle. The mantle makes a liquid that hardens into the shell. The mantle lets out liquid slowly over time. This way, the conch's shell grows larger and thicker as the conch grows.

This is what the conch snail looks like outside of its shell.

Conches' thick shells keep them safe. This queen conch is peering out of its shell.

Conches come in many sizes, shapes, and colors. The queen conch can grow to be about 1 foot (.3 m) long and weigh 5 pounds (2.3 kg). The inside of its shell can be pink, yellow, or orange.

All gastropods have a single foot they use to get around. A conch uses its foot to slowly move around on the ocean floor. The foot is a muscular organ that spreads out under the conch's body.

Queen conches do move, but very slowly. This queen conch is moving along the sandy bottom of the Atlantic Ocean, near the Bahamas.

Here, you can see the foot and eye coming out of this queen conch's shell.

The queen conch is known for hopping with its foot. Scientists think queen conches hop so that they will not leave a trail in the sand for predators to follow. Queen conches can travel about 1 mile (1.6 km) over two months.

Queen conches are most active at night. This is when they look for food. During the day, they often find hiding places in coral reefs or rocky ledges. They also hide by burying themselves under sand.

Conch Facts!

1. The queen conch has a claw-shaped horn at the end of its foot. Conches use this horn to help them move and free themselves from predators.

2. Conches' shells are made from a hard material called calcium carbonate.

3. Spider conches have long spines, that stick out along the lip of their shells. The spines almost look like spider legs!

4. Fighting conches are known for attacking other animals.

5. The queen conch sometimes makes a pearl. The pearl can be a pink or gold color. It is made from the same material as the conch's shell.

6. Although they generally live in shallower waters, queen conches have been found in water up to 500 feet (152 m) deep.

7. Conches can pull themselves back into their shells to hide, as other snails can.

8. Conches have two pairs of **tentacles** on their heads. Their eyes are at the end of the longer pair of tentacles. The shorter pair is used for smelling and feeling.

Eggs and Larvae

Female conches reproduce, or make more conches, with the help of male conches. After **mating**, female queen conches lay a long, sticky string of eggs, called an egg mass. The egg mass holds up to 400,000 eggs and can be more than 100 feet (30.5 m) long! After about five days, tiny **larvae** hatch from the eggs.

Young conches and larvae are at risk of being eaten by predators. Full grown conches, like these, are protected by their tough shells.

Plankton float in the ocean and are so small they cannot be seen. Many sea animals eat plankton, including conch larvae.

The larvae float through the ocean waters for their first few weeks. They eat tiny plants called plankton. Then, they settle on the ocean floor, where they change into small conches. However, it can take 3 to 4 years for a queen conch to reach full size. They can live for 20 to 40 years in the wild!

Plant Eaters

Conches eat mostly plants. Their diet includes **algae**, sea grasses, and **bacteria** that grow on sea grasses. Sometimes, conches swallow pieces of sand and gravel that are covered in algae. Conches will also eat tiny pieces of dead plants and animals that sink to the ocean floor.

Sea grasses and the bacteria that grow on them are a big part of the conch's diet.

Conches sometimes eat detritus. Detritus is decomposing plants or animals that have sunk to the bottom of the sea.

Conches move around the ocean floor at night looking for food. They can feel and smell food using the tentacles on their heads. Conches suck up their food with a tubelike mouth called a proboscis. Then, they grind the food up using their radulas. The radula is an organ covered in thousands of tiny, sharp teeth called denticles.

Conch Predators

Young conches are much smaller than adult conches. They also have thinner shells. This makes it easier for ocean predators to eat them. Young conches often bury themselves in the sand to hide from predators.

Adult conches are kept safe from many predators by their thick shells. However, there are ocean predators that are able to eat animals with thick shells. These include loggerhead sea turtles, nurse sharks, and stingrays.

Conches have very hard shells, but the shells do not keep them safe from all predators. Tiger sharks, such as this one, can easily crack open a conch shell.

The bluespotted ribbontail ray is not only a danger to conches. It has venomous spines on its tail that can injure humans!

When a predator comes close, conches pull back into their shells. They can also use the claws at the end of their feet to try to pry themselves loose from a predator's mouth.

People and Conches

Conches are fished by people around the world. In countries around the Caribbean Sea and the Gulf of Mexico, people fish for the large queen conch. The queen conch is caught for its meat and its beautiful shell. People eat queen conch meat all around the Caribbean. Some conch dishes include chowder and fritters. The meat can also be used as fishing bait.

Blowing on a conch shell can make a loud sound. Conch shells are used as musical instruments.

Conch meat is a popular food in the Caribbean. This man is preparing conch meat for a restaurant in Turks and Caicos.

Conch shells are made into jewelry and other decorations. Native peoples have also used conch shells to make musical instruments, cooking pots, knives, hooks, and buttons. Today, people also keep different kinds of conches in aquariums as pets.

For many years, there were no laws to keep people from catching too many queen conches. **Overfishing** has made their numbers much smaller than they should be. Ocean pollution has also hurt queen conches' habitats.

Today, governments and wildlife groups are working to keep the queen conch safe from dying out. It is important to take care of the Earth and its animals. That way, conches will be around for many years to come.

Glossary

algae (AL-jee) Plantlike living things without roots or stems that live in water.

bacteria (bak-TIR-ee-uh) Tiny living things that cannot be seen with the eye alone.

family (FAM-lee) The scientific name for a large group of plants or animals that are alike in some ways.

gastropods (GAS-truh-podz) Kinds of soft-bellied mollusks, or shellfish, that each have a head and a single foot. Their name means "belly footed."

habitats (HA-buh-tats) The surroundings where animals or plants naturally live.

larvae (LAHR-vee) Insects in the early life stage in which they have a wormlike form.

marine (muh-REEN) Having to do with the sea.

mating (MAYT-ing) Joining together to make babies.

organ (AWR-gun) A part inside the body that does a job.

overfishing (oh-ver-FISH-ing) Catching too many fish.

predators (PREH-duh-terz) Animals that kill other animals for food.

shallow (SHA-loh) Not deep.

spiral (SPY-rul) A curved or curled design.

tentacles (TEN-tih-kulz) Long, thin growths used to touch, hold, or move that are usually on the heads or near the mouths of animals.

Index

Websites

Due to the changing nature of Internet links, PowerKids Press has developed an online list of websites related to the subject of this book. This site is updated regularly. Please use this link to access the list: www.powerkidslinks.com/aaa/conch/